KEIGHLEY TRAMWAYS AND TROLLEYBUSES

Barry M Marsden

Series editor Robert J Harley

Cover pictures: Please see captions 20 (front) and 89 (back).

Cover colours: All Keighley electric vehicles were painted crimson and white.

Published August 2006

ISBN 1 904474 83 7

© Middleton Press, 2006

Design Deborah Esher

Published by
       Middleton Press
       Easebourne Lane
       Midhurst, West Sussex
       GU29 9AZ
Tel: 01730 813169
Fax: 01730 812601
Email: info@middletonpress.co.uk
www.middletonpress.co.uk

Printed & bound by Biddles Ltd, Kings Lynn

CONTENTS

HORSE CARS

Plan of the Horse Car System	1	North Street	5
Utley Terminus	2	Ingrow Terminus	6
Skipton Road	4		

ELECTRIC TRAMS

Plan of the Electric Tram System	8	Bridge Street	33
Board of Trade Inspection	9	South Street	34
Opening Day	11	Ingrow Terminus	41
Utley Terminus	16	Cavendish Street	44
Skipton Road	18	Bradford Road	48
North Street	24	Decorated Cars	49

CEDES-STOLL TROLLEYBUSES

Plan of the Trolleybus Systems	51	Utley Terminus	56
Ingrow Terminus	52	Hawkcliffe	61
Cross Roads	53	Sutton-in-Craven	62
Oakworth	55		

KEIGHLEY TROLLEYBUSES

Fleet Vehicles	63	Ingrow Terminus	88
Utley Terminus	70	Cavendish Street	94
Skipton Road	76	Bradford Road	99
North Street	78	Stockbridge Terminus	103
Church Street	83	Last Day	109
High Street	85	Survivors	114

INTRODUCTION AND ACKNOWLEDGEMENTS

I came to live in Yorkshire from my native Derbyshire in 1975, and settled in a village on the edge of Ilkley Moor. The town of Keighley is just a few minutes away from our home, and though I was aware of its interesting transport history, it was only through the recent generosity of Stanley King that I was able to gather sufficient images to make up a viable volume on the subject. Keighley was associated with all forms of early public transport, commencing with horse and electric tramcars, before becoming one of the earliest experimenters with the trolleybus to serve its outlying districts. It later replaced its trams with further trolleybuses (always known as 'tracklesses' in the township), but abandoned electric transport as early as 1932 in favour of the all-powerful motorbus.

The photographs illustrating this book come mainly from the collection of Stanley King who documented the town's public transportation in his pioneering *Keighley Corporation Transport* of 1964. Images have also been supplied through the kindness of Robin Symonds and the National Trolleybus Association (including the Harold Brearley Collection), whilst other illustrations are by courtesy of Graham Mitchell and the Keighley Bus Museum Trust, G. Crowther and Colin Routh. Vehicle drawings have been kindly supplied by Terry Russell and tickets by Godfrey Croughton to whom I tender my grateful thanks.

GEOGRAPHICAL SETTING

Keighley is situated in the Aire Valley between the Rivers Aire and Worth, around a mile south of the confluence between the two waterways. The town was served by the Leeds-Liverpool Canal, and later the Midland Railway. Lying ten miles/16km north-west of the City of Bradford, it developed as an outpost of the West Riding industrial complex. The steam trains of the Keighley & Worth Valley Railway are a major tourist attraction in the locality.

HISTORICAL BACKGROUND

The first tramway to be constructed in Keighley was a horse drawn one (owned by the Keighley Tramways Company Ltd.), promoted by a consortium of local businessmen and consisting of a single track line of 4ft/1219mm gauge running south from Utley through the town centre, and ending at Ingrow. It was 2.28 miles/3.6km long and was served by seven open-top double-deck trams built by Starbuck. The North Street-Ingrow section opened on 2nd May 1889, with the Utley-North Street half following on 18th December. Very short extensions to the line were completed in 1897, to the Roebuck Inn at Utley and to the new Ingrow bridge which crossed the River Worth. The two parts of the undertaking were normally worked as two separate routes. The livery carried by the tramcars is unfortunately not known.

Never a viable facility, the Company sold the track to Keighley Corporation on 25th November 1896 for the nominal sum of £5, and leased it back for 13 years. On 15th January 1901 the Corporation, who wished to extend and electrify the concern, purchased it and took over the running on 21st September. The Company was thereupon wound up, and the tramway carried on under its new ownership until 1904 when the line was closed for complete reconstruction and electrification.

The Corporation planned to extend the line by means of a branch to Stockbridge to the north-east, hoping for an eventual link with Shipley and Bradford, but the junction was never destined to happen. The old horse route was relaid as double track, again at a 4ft gauge, whilst the Stockbridge section was twin-track from the Mechanics' Institute in North Street as far as the Midland Railway Station, where it continued as single track with passing loops as far as Victoria Park on Bradford Road.

The initial rolling stock consisted of eight open top Brush cars, joined by a further two in 1905, after the Stockbridge branch had been extended half a mile as far as Dale Street on 10th February of that year, giving the undertaking a total track length of 3.44 miles/5.5km, most of which was fairly level, with no significant inclines. Running on Brush 21E trucks with a six-foot/1828mm wheelbase, the trams were painted in crimson and white. In 1906 two balcony top-covered vehicles joined the fleet, and between 1910-1912 all the open toppers had their upper decks retrospectively covered over.

By 1913, the growing expense of maintaining the tramway led the Corporation to experiment with early trolleybuses to service the outlying districts, but the First World War killed off any prospects of extending the lines. Faced with the prospect of relaying the tramtrack in the 1920s, the powers-that-be decided to abandon the system and replace the through-town routes with trolleybuses. Accordingly the Utley line closed on 20th August 1924, followed by Stockbridge on 20th November, and Ingrow on 13th December, though 2-3 cars maintained a workmen's service on this section until the 17th of the month. Keighley thus had the dubious distinction of being the first local authority to replace its complete tram system with trolley vehicles.

In 1911, Keighley's Tramways Manager, Harry Webber, opted for trolleybuses to operate three routes in the township's outlying districts, obviously influenced by nearby Bradford and Leeds who were experimenting with this type of vehicle. Despite much opposition from local authorities who were worried by the effects of these conveyances on their roads, and from the railways who feared the competition, Keighley Corporation applied for powers to run trackless cars from Utley to Sutton-in-Craven, from Stockbridge to Nab Wood, from the town centre to Oakworth, and from Ingrow via Cross Roads to Oxenhope. The Stockbridge route was later abandoned, but the others remained in the Bill, which became law in August 1912.

During 1912, the Corporation examined the various railless systems, and Webber, in what must have been a moment of delusion, opted for the Austrian Cedes-Stoll method of propulsion, no doubt seduced by their agent's (Trackless Trolley Ltd of London) offer to erect one mile 1400 yards/2.8km of overhead line from Ingrow to Hebden Road end, and to provide one car on a free three month trial, using their over-running, four wheel trolley on the twin wires, which was linked to the trackless by a towed flexible cable. If the test proved unsuccessful they undertook to adapt the wiring for the more conventional twin boom system. Just why Webber settled for the Heath-Robinson Cedes power supply, when perfectly good paired trolleyboom engineering had already been perfected remains a mystery, but he remained an aficionado of the flawed current collection method throughout his managership. The only other municipality misguided enough to adopt the Cedes-Stoll mode was Aberdare, with equally unsatisfactory results.

The official inspection of the Cross Roads route took place on 24th April 1913, and the service began on 3rd May using an Austrian single-deck trolleybus which had operated in Vienna and had subsequently been demonstrated at West Ham. Keighley Corporation duly bought the car and gave it the number '0'. Two more cars (1 and 2) were ordered from Trackless Trolley and in October the Corporation accepted a Cedes tender for 6 miles 1540 yards/11km of overhead line on the Sutton and Oakworth routes, and for four more trackless cars equipped with Dodson bodywork. Two further vehicles were ordered later, and the succeeding trolleybuses were provided with more powerful motors to cope with the hillier sections of line.

The new overhead was carried on distinctive continental style lattice poles, and the two new routes were inspected on 15th December 1914. The Oakworth service began immediately, but the Sutton one was postponed until the final cars were delivered, and did not commence until the following January, though full operations took until the end of February to begin. The Cross Roads-Oxenhope extension was completed in 1916, using surplus equipment from a demonstration line installed at Hove, and the trial run took place on 29th June. An official inspection took place on 2nd July, but following County Council objections, Keighley reluctantly agreed not to run to the village until after the war.

A measure of the danger of using non-British equipment was underlined when the Cedes company was compulsorily wound up by the government in 1916 as an enemy concern, and the Corporation had to locate new sources of supply for gear and motors. At the sale of Cedes plant and effects they purchased the Cedes open top, double decker used at Hove. This vehicle was the first double deck trolleybus ever built, and was given the number 9. A dearth of spares and new equipment caused by the war and the demise of Trackless Trolleys rendered the Cedes service thoroughly disordered, and by April 1920 only one car remained in service, on the Cross Roads route. The Sutton route reopened shortly afterwards and a single trolleybus ran part of the way to Oakworth in July, after a two year gap, but the vehicle broke down a few days later.

A determined effort to reinvigorate the services in 1921 led to four renovated tracklesses operating to Cross Roads and along the Sutton line as far as Crosshills commencing on 25th March, and the Oxenhope extension was finally opened. Sadly, all was not well, and the Oxenhope line closed on 24th October, followed by Oakworth on 2nd December.

In 1923 the Council agreed to replace the ageing tramcars with a modern trolleybus fleet, and the resulting Bill received the Royal Assent in July 1924. Keighley also hoped to restart the practically moribund Sutton and Cross Roads lines by utilising modern trackless vehicles, but the former service ran for the last time on 23rd May 1924. The latter route staggered on still using the Cedes collection equipment but finally succumbed on 3rd May 1926. Parodying Shakespeare's *King Lear*, one might comment 'the wonder is it hath endured so long.'

The Utley trams were superseded by trolleybuses on 20th August 1924, using new single-deckers 1-4, which comprised bodies rescued from the Cedes vehicles, mounted on new Straker chassis, and using the same livery as the trams. The Stockbridge line began working on 21st November, followed by Ingrow on 14th December. The new fleet included five double deck Strakers (5-10) with Brush bodies, and four new single deckers (11-14) with bodies supplied by the same company. Four more double deckers (15-18) completed the line up in 1925.

During the 1920s the growing need for through routes and co-ordinated services into surrounding areas, plus motorbus competition, led, in 1931-2, to plans for a new company, to be owned jointly by Keighley Corporation and the West Yorkshire Road Car Company. This programme envisaged the demise of the trolleybuses, and in August 1932 the Council announced that the vehicles would be replaced at the end of the month by a bus service until the joint company began operations. Accordingly, on the evening of 31st August a crowd assembled by the Institute to witness the closure of the electric system. The official last trackless was No.17, followed by the final service cars which included Nos. 15 and 16, the last to enter Utley Depot.

Sadly the Corporation could not have anticipated that its Straker trolleybuses would have been rendered so speedily obsolete by the rapid technical advances in vehicle design during the later 1920s. Although only eight years old when scrapped, they looked obsolete and could hardly stand comparison with the newer vehicles constantly placed in service by their competitors, as they gained a stranglehold on the Corporation's routes. Fortunately two of the tracklesses still survive, double deck No.5, now kept at the Keighley Bus Museum, and single deck No.12, preserved at Beamish.

HORSE CARS

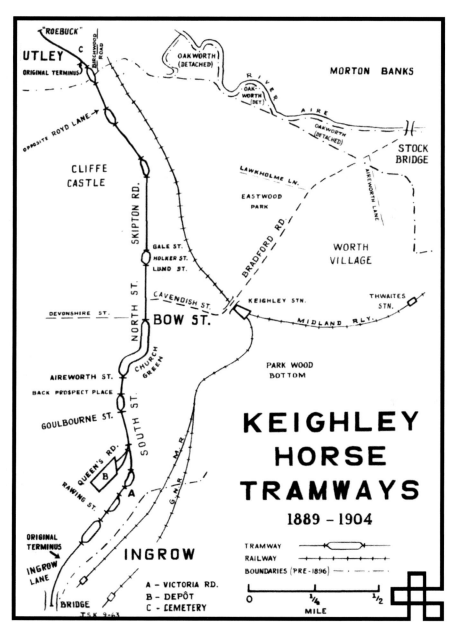

1.   The horse tram route, inaugurated in 1889 was a simple single line with turnouts, running due south from Utley to Ingrow, and covering some 2.44 miles/ 3.9km. The depot on Queen's Road was later extended for the electric car fleet.

UTLEY TERMINUS

2.   The terminus was extended to the Roebuck Inn in 1897 and this view shows Car 1, one of the larger 44 seat vehicles, outside the public house. The horses seem well groomed though the crew look a pair of desperate characters, doubtless a result of the 100 hour week they had to work! Note the tramways logo on the rocker panel, and the fancy scrolling on the waist.

3.   Another image taken outside the Roebuck of a similar tram, though the number is missing from the waist panel. The horses are turned for the return trip to the Institute, with a disparate group of passengers including the gent in the fancy hat standing behind the rear staircase.

SKIPTON ROAD

4.   A well loaded tram, running along the single track on a thoroughfare almost bereft of other road traffic, pauses at the gate to Cliffe Castle on its way into town.

NORTH STREET

5.　　　One of the larger trams passes the façade of the Mechanics' Institute on its way to Ingrow with Cavendish Street visible on the right. To the left of the driver's right shoulder is the large red bullseye illuminated from inside the saloon by a paraffin lamp.

INGROW TERMINUS

6.   Ingrow Bridge, crossing the River Worth, is here seen looking towards town with the tram track curving away in the distance. The tram shelter on the left is now preserved in Keighley Bus Museum, whilst the bulk of St. Johns Church looms up at the top left of the picture.

7.   One of the lighter trams, No.8, pauses at Ingrow in a shot taken from the opposite direction to the last. Note the lack of a rocker panel logo, suggesting that the facility was now a Corporation owned one. The horse on the left appears to be enjoying a good joke!

THE ELECTRIC TRAMS

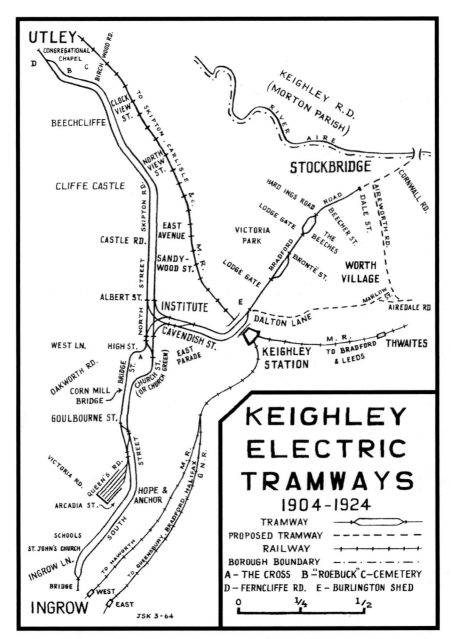

The following labels appear on the map:

UTLEY · CONGREGATIONAL CHAPEL · D · B · C · BIRCH WOOD RD. · CLOCK VIEW ST. · TO SKIPTON · CARLISLE & c. · BEECHCLIFFE · NORTH VIEW ST. · CLIFFE CASTLE · SKIPTON RD. · EAST AVENUE · CASTLE RD. · SANDY-WOOD ST. · ALBERT ST. · INSTITUTE · NORTH STREET · M.R. · CAVENDISH ST. · WEST LN. · HIGH ST. · A · EAST PARADE · OAKWORTH RD. · BRIDGE ST. · CHURCH ST. (OR CHURCH GREEN) · CORN MILL BRIDGE · GOULBOURNE ST. · VICTORIA RD. · QUEEN'S RD. · STREET · HOPE & ANCHOR · ARCADIA ST. · SCHOOLS · ST. JOHN'S CHURCH · INGROW LN. · SOUTH · TO HAWORTH · TO QUEENSBURY, BRADFORD, HALIFAX · M.R. · G.N.R. · BRIDGE · WEST · EAST · INGROW · JSK 3-64

KEIGHLEY R.D. (MORTON PARISH) · RIVER AIRE · STOCKBRIDGE · CORNWALL RD. · HARD INGS ROAD · ROAD · DALE ST. · BEECHER ST. · AIREWORTH RD. · LODGE GATE · THE BEECHES · VICTORIA PARK · BRADFORD ST. · BRONTE ST. · WORTH VILLAGE · LODGE GATE · MARLOW ST. · AIREDALE RD · DALTON LANE · E · KEIGHLEY STATION · M.R. TO BRADFORD & LEEDS · THWAITES · BURLINGTON SHED

KEIGHLEY ELECTRIC TRAMWAYS 1904-1924

TRAMWAY
PROPOSED TRAMWAY
RAILWAY
BOROUGH BOUNDARY
A – THE CROSS B –"ROEBUCK" C–CEMETERY
D – FERNCLIFFE RD. E – BURLINGTON SHED
0   ¼   ½

8.   The plan of the electric tramway shows the Stockbridge extension, running down Cavendish Street from the Institute and heading north-east along Bradford Road. The route was largely double track, apart from the single line and loop stretch beyond Dalton Lane.

THE BOARD OF TRADE INSPECTION

9.   On the morning of 12th October a considerable party of officials and others boarded Car 3, here pictured, and Car 2 following on behind. Never can so many bowler hats have been gathered together in Keighley – at least 21 examples of this type of headgear are represented in the shot. The image picks out the Corporation livery, in pristine condition, to perfection, and points up the salient features of the Brush 6ft truck, a blatant copy of the American Brill 21E.

10.　　　Car 6 is seen at Utley and points towards Steeton - presumably another image from the BoT inspection. The track points behind the tram are receiving some attention, whilst the trolley pole is clearly running on the wrong overhead line. Note the destination blind reading MECHANICS INSTITUTE

OPENING DAY

11.   A whole series of photographs of the opening day were taken by busy cameramen, mostly at the Utley terminus. Here Car 2 is the subject, carefully protected by two guardians of the law. Of amusing interest is the obviously fake laurel bush on the right, drawn in to hide an unsightly outside privy!

12.   Car 8, manned by dignitaries and Brush staff, and accompanied by posed pedestrians and a cyclist, is shown outside Utley Congregational Chapel, later demolished and now occupied by the Dalesman Hotel. The indicator blind is of interest, as it shows an obscure locality identified as NEW ROAD SIDE.

13. A well patronised and decorated Car 3 is depicted at Utley, though the latter description is probably overstated in view of the dearth of bunting and flags. The vehicle was reputedly driven by Alderman Clough, and a goodly crowd of youngsters has been gathered by the photographer for his shot, some of whom obviously could not keep still! The twin track merging into one terminal line can be seen behind the tram. On this vehicle the destination reads RAILWAY STATION.

14. The same tram is pictured at the same venue perhaps later in the day, as the posing dignitaries on the front platform have been replaced by a more proficient looking crew. Utley Congregational Chapel shows up well on the right, with some solidly built houses lining Skipton Road.

15. We observe one final shot of opening day, with SPECIAL CAR 1 posed by the chapel. Another cyclist has joined the onlookers, together with several ladies in fine hats. The passengers look more like Brush officials than fare paying riders.

UTLEY TERMINUS

16.   Car 10, one of the 1905 batch lays over at Utley with the trolleyboom already swung for the return to Ingrow. The motorman and conductor pose for the camera on what is, in effect, the rear platform. The 9-10 vehicles were slightly different to the earlier ones – note in particular the air vents over the windows and the wooden handrail running round the top of the dash panel. The INGROW destination on the indicator blinds has been reinforced with a board slid into the base of the central window.

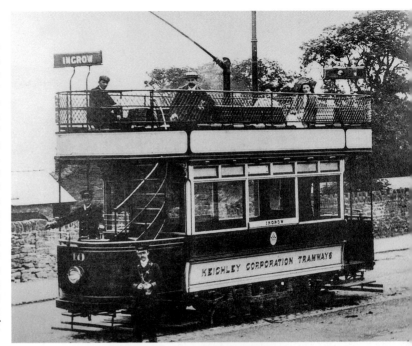

17.   Car 10 again, occupies the same position as Car 2 in picture 11. This time the privy on the right can be appreciated in its full glory! This image was obviously taken at the same time as the last, as both crewmen are the same. The conductor has not yet swung the backs of the top deck garden seats to face the direction of travel.

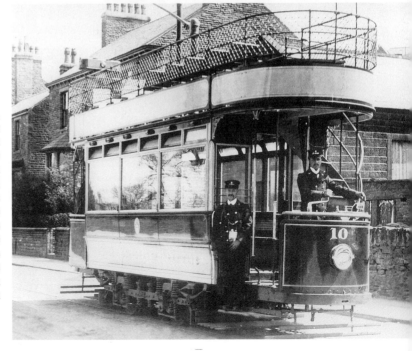

18.   Car 4 opposite the Roebuck, a 1924 vista taken after one set of tramlines had been removed, and the traction poles for the trolleybuses were in the process of erection by the workmen visible in shot. The tram had long been top-covered, and only differed from Balcony cars 11-12 in the positioning of the indicator blind. Its placement below the vestibule roof must have been inconvenient for the taller motormen.

19.   Outside Utley Cemetery gate Car 11, en route for the MECHANICS, stops for the camera, whilst labourers lift the tramtrack and raise the posts for the trackless overhead in another 1924 image near the end of the electric tram service.

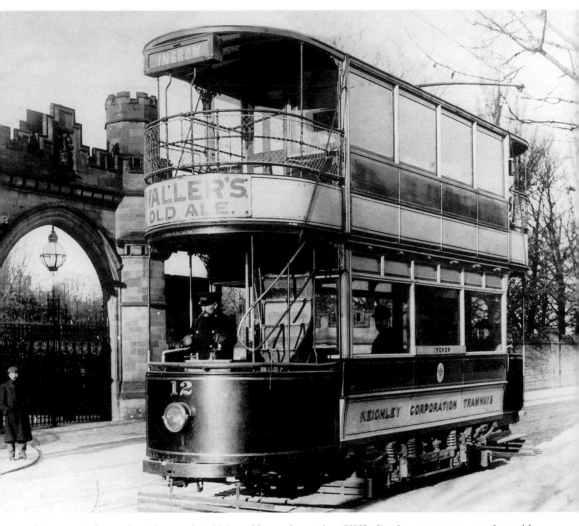

20.   Balcony Car 12, new in 1906, and here pictured at Cliffe Castle gates, was, together with No.11, the first top covered tram in the fleet. Note that the upper deck has four windows per side, but only three in the saloon. When the rest of the vehicles received top covers, they were supplied with three upper deck windows on each side. The destination blinds were fixed below the open top deck canopies at each end of the tram.

21.   Track lifting proceeds along Skipton Road in June 1924, with Castle Road marked by the line of houses in the background. One set of lines was intitially removed, leaving the trams only a single track to use, a recipe which led to much congestion and annoyance to other road users. The view picks out well the 18in wide layer of paving outside the tracks which was unfairly left for tramways departments to maintain.

22.   Car 5 pauses on its way to Ingrow, with Spring Gardens Lane visible on the left, whilst children gather for the photographer in a spot they would be extremely foolhardy to loiter in today. Practically all the Keighley overhead wiring was carried on twin poles and span wire, whose details show up clearly in this postcard.

23.   One of the 9-10 series trams halts near Holker Street on 3rd September 1905, carrying members of a French delegation, presumably connected with the recent Anglo-French Entente Cordiale if the portrait of King Edward VII on the front of the car is anything to go by. The Tramways Department have obviously made a better fist of decorating the vehicle than they did for the opening of the system. The gent with the umbrella on the front platform has been identified as the Tramways Manager, Mr John Bamber.

NORTH STREET

24.   A view taken looking due south along North Street, shows the double track, and twin pole and span wire arrangement of the overhead. The imposing clock tower of the Mechanics' Institute can be seen just right of centre, whilst a tram can be glimpsed in the far distance.

25.   Looking in the opposite direction Car 3, now top covered, stops outside the public library on the left. The impressive cupola above the tram crowns a building on the corner of Albert Street, now a branch of Wetherspoons. Of interest is the indicator blind, which was usually set above the driver's platform on the 1-10 series vehicles. Though the postcard is titled Skipton Road, it is of course North Street.

26.   Car 3 is seen again, this time travelling in the opposite direction in much the same place, with the blind evidently reset above the lower vestibule. The tram was on one of its last journeys, on 13th December 1924, utilising the new trackless overhead, whilst the front platform seems unduly crowded with passengers.

27.   Tracklaying is here seen taking place against the backdrop of the Institute, during the summer of 1904. The twin rails were laid on a concrete bed, and the operations appear to be keenly watched by a number of interested idlers. The through-town operation must have caused severe disruption to local traffic. Note the 'Y' junction leading into Cavendish Street on the right of the picture.

←———

28.   Car 1 passes the Institute on its way to Ingrow, with Cavendish Street visible on the right, in more-or-less the same vantage point as the last illustration. Note the two splendidly behatted ladies riding on the upper deck.

←———

29.   Three types of Keighley Corporation Transport vehicles are here depicted in this 17th December 1924 image, taken on the very last day of tramcar operation. To the left of Car 6, which is running under trolleybus wiring, is Leyland SG9 motorbus No.28 (always known as 'Big Bertha'), whilst one of the new Straker double-deck trackless vehicles is caught heading up Cavendish Street. It awaits the point-duty policeman's permission to proceed. The splendid clock tower of the Institute looms above the tram.

30.   Chaos reigns supreme in this Coronation Day shot taken on 21st June 1911, at the North Street-Cavendish Street intersection. Three top covered cars jockey for position on the 'Y' junction, with trams loading for Stockbridge and Utley on the left, whilst Car 10 is about to head off for Ingrow. On the far right, Car 1, also on the Utley run, remains an open topper. Note the stylish looking motor car at the bottom left, vainly seeking a way through the thronged roadway.

31.   A final look at the North Street-Cavendish Street junction, with Car 11 on the Ingrow run and Car 6 heading for Stockbridge on the right. The trees, in full leaf, suggest a summer 1924 date, and the stately lines of the Institute serve to remind us of the fine building it once was. It was torn down, together with a church, to erect a fairly hideous 1960s replacement - Keighley Technical College - a far less distinguished edifice.

32.   Further south down North Street, Car 8 pauses just behind the facing crossover visible behind the schoolboy walking just to the right of the tram. The Institute tower can be seen in the distance, whilst in the foreground the tracks begin to diverge – vehicles to Ingrow took the line on the right, whilst those for Utley ran on the left hand track. Note the splendid early automobile on the right, and the car stop sign on the left hand traction pole.

BRIDGE STREET

33.   Dilapidated tram track is depicted at Corn Mill Bridge on Bridge Street, just before abandonment. The line can be seen curving right into High Street on the way to Utley. Note how the tracks have sunk in the roadway; here the narrowness of the street makes its maintenance the responsibility of the Tramways Department as the setts outside the lines were less than 18ins/ 457mm from the kerb.

34.   Car 3 is here pictured near the depot, which is just off shot to the left. The houses are fronting Apsley Street and the Italianate tower of the long demolished St Peter's Church dominates the background. The SPECIAL CAR destination and bowler-hatted motorman suggest another opening day scene.

35.   Twenty-two members of the Tramways staff line up at the depot in front of one of the 9-10 series cars around 1910. By this time, advertisements have begun to appear on the rolling stock, mostly concerning local firms, but whatever happened to Bensdorp's Cocoa?

36.   Another depot image, this time relating to the end of 1916, when the first motorwoman was employed by the Corporation. Conductresses, like the five pictured in rather fetching hats, were recruited from the previous April. The motorwoman can be seen on the left, wearing a rather shapeless peaked cap.

38.   This singular postcard portrays an accident to three children on 6th February 1907, when they were caught by the lifeguard tray of Car 7 on a snowy winter night when their sledge ran down Rawling Street on the left, straight under the passing tram. None were fortunately seriously hurt, but the artist deployed much licence in this supposed depiction. The houses on Rawling Street do not have front gardens, and the church on the right simply never existed. A considerable number of toffs must have been enjoying a top deck ride judging by the selection of top hats being worn, and why, on a chilly dark winter's night was no one wearing appropriate clothing? Finally if the tram was heading for Utley, it is facing the wrong way!

37.   The tram shed still exists, situated between Queen's Road on the right and Arcadia Street on the left. Sadly no carved lettering above the door lintel indicates its former purpose.

39.   This image shows the very last length of tram track being ceremonially lifted on South Street on 4th February 1926, in the presence of civic dignitaries, including the Mayor, Alderman A. Smith, the diminutive figure at the centre of the photograph.

INGROW TERMINUS

40.   The first tramcar to Ingrow, Car 1, ⟶
took part in a trial run from the depot on 16th   41.   The decorated car carrying the French
September 1904. It was staffed by councillors   delegation, during its tour of Keighley on 3rd
and Brush Company employees, and was   September 1905, arrives at Ingrow. Upper deck
greeted by an enthusiastic crowd. The roof of St   riders enthusiastically doff their hats to passers-
John's Church can be seen at the top left.   by.

⟶
42.   A fine view of Car 10 at Ingrow, pictured departing for Utley, again shows well the
twin pole and span wire arrangement of the overhead, whilst St John's Church dominates the
background. The singular gents' toilet on the left, thoughtfully crowned by a streetlamp, was
adjacent to a horse trough which occasionally became live, and caused drinking equines to kick
out, but it is not known whether the toilet dispensed similar electric shocks!

43.   Another Ingrow image, taken this time from the opposite direction, shows Car 1 on a dark, dismal day. The circular urinal and drinking trough can be seen to the right of the tram.

CAVENDISH STREET

44.　　　More mayhem has been caught on camera at the top end of Cavendish Street, again almost certainly on Coronation Day 1911. The imposing frontage of the public library, built in 1902, is visible in the background. Car 10 is heading this time for Stockbridge. An open topper and a balcony tram jostle for position on the right, whilst the car crews indulge in desultory chit-chat. Note the vast crowds thronging the roadway in this central part of town.

45.   Car 8, Utley bound at the top of the same street, shows off its brand new paint job and equally new Brill 21E truck in this 1922 photograph. The truck was purchased at a cost of £125. The window bills advertise anniversary church services. On the right, Car 9 prepares to head for Stockbridge. Note the pointsman busy in front of the latter vehicle.

46.   Keighley's very last tramcar, Car 6, uses trolleybus running wire as it prepares to turn left at the western end of Cavendish Street on its final journey to Ingrow on 17th December 1924.

47.   Balcony Car 11 ascends the street sometime around 1912. Note the arc lamp and stop sign on the left hand traction pole, and the continuous glass veranda on the right, which still survives. In this scene multitudes of shoppers can be seen thronging the pavements.

BRADFORD ROAD

48.   Unfortunately the Stockbridge route was poorly served by contemporary cameramen, and this scene taken at Dalton Lane Top at rush-hour will have to suffice. Here Cars 5 and 1 await the midday mill and factory crowds circa 1923. Again the window bills advertise anniversary church services.

DECORATED CARS

49.   Decorated tramcars were a tradition among municipalities, and this splendid example, bedizened for King George V's Coronation, is a credit to the Keighley staff. The vehicle, fitted with some 600 light bulbs, ran 6d/2.5p circular evening tours from 22nd June until 1st July, and was evidently a great success.

50.   In a rather more sombre vein this balcony tram was decked out in 1914 for Lord Kitchener's recruiting campaign, calling on patriotic Yorkshiremen to join up at Keighley Drill Hall. The photograph was probably taken inside the South Street depot.

KEIGHLEY CORP. TRAMWAYS DOUBLE DECK "TRACKLESS"		Overall length: 24'
Chassis: Straker-"Squire" Body: Brush 1924. Fleet No: 5-10 & 15-18.	Scale: 4 mm = 1Foot.	Body length: 23'6" Saloon length: 15'6" Body width: 7' Wheelbase: 14'6"
DRAWING No. TB46		

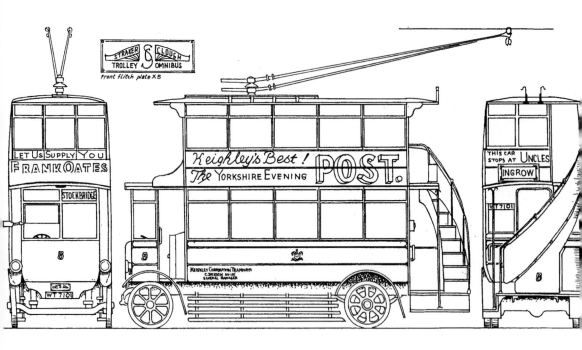

Front flitch plate × 5

LET Us SUPPLY YOU

FRANK OATES

STOCKBRIDGE

Keighley's Best! POST.

The YORKSHIRE EVENING

THIS CAR STOPS AT UNCLES

INGROW

KEIGHLEY CORPORATION TRAMWAYS C.JACKSON A.M.I.E.E & GENERAL MANAGER

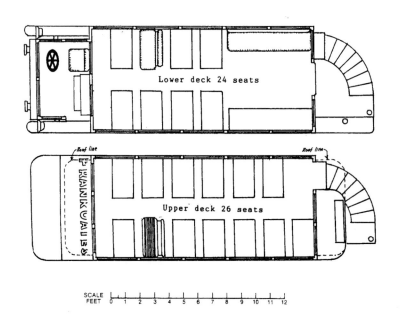

Lower deck 24 seats

Roof line   Roof line

Upper deck 26 seats

SCALE FEET	0 1 2 3 4 5 6 7 8 9 10 11 12

DRAWN BY:-   K.A.Allbon 02/03   AND KINDLY MADE AVAILABLE THROUGH:-
TERRY RUSSELL, "CHACESIDE", ST. LEONARDS PARK, HORSHAM, W.SUSSEX. RH13 6EG.
SEND 4 FIRST CLASS STAMPS FOR COMPLETE LIST OF PUBLIC TRANSPORT DRAWINGS.

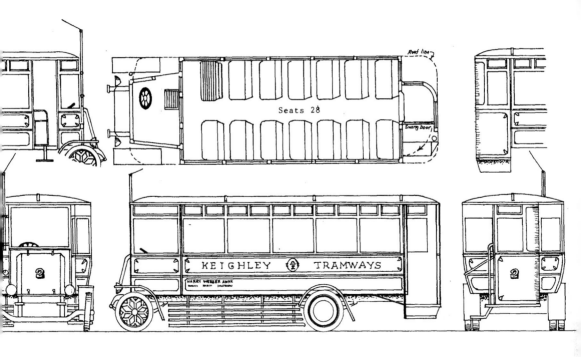

KEIGHLEY  TRAMWAYS

KEIGHLEY CORP. TRAMWAYS SINGLE DECK "TRACKLESS"	
Chassis: Cedes–Stoll. Body: Dobson 1914. Fleet No: 1-8. (later 51-58.)	Scale: 4 mm = 1 Foot.
DRAWING No. TB45	

```
Overall length:   22'6"
Body     length:   21'
Saloon   length:   15'
Body width:         7'3"
Wheelbase:        12'8"
```

SCALE
FEET   0 1 2 3 4 5 6 7 8 9 10 11 12

DRAWN BY:-   K.A.Allbon 02/03   AND KINDLY MADE AVAILABLE THROUGH:-
TERRY RUSSELL, "CHACESIDE", ST. LEONARDS PARK, HORSHAM, W.SUSSEX. RH13 6EG.
SEND 4 FIRST CLASS STAMPS FOR COMPLETE LIST OF PUBLIC TRANSPORT DRAWINGS.

EVERYTHING You NEED TYLER'S
Take This Car to

THE CEDES-STOLL
TROLLEYBUSES

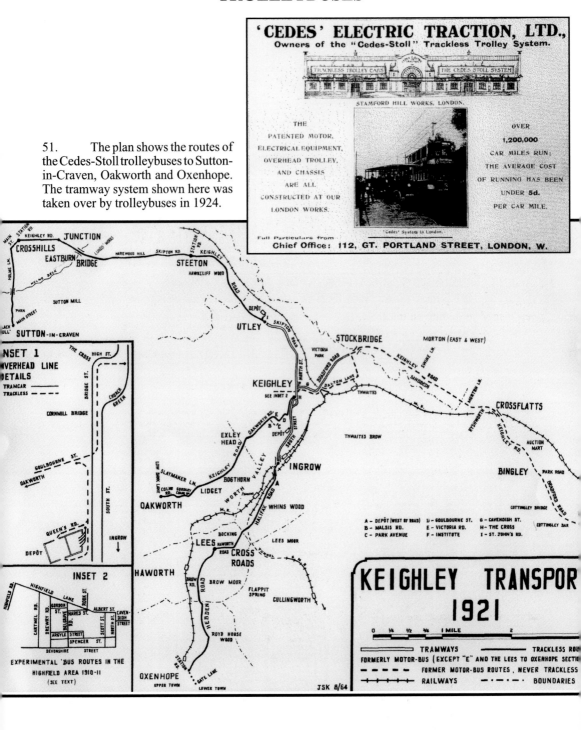

51.   The plan shows the routes of the Cedes-Stoll trolleybuses to Sutton-in-Craven, Oakworth and Oxenhope. The tramway system shown here was taken over by trolleybuses in 1924.

'CEDES' ELECTRIC TRACTION, LTD.,
Owners of the "Cedes-Stoll" Trackless Trolley System.

TRACKLESS TROLLEY CARS   THE CEDES STOLL SYSTEM

STAMFORD HILL WORKS, LONDON.

THE
PATENTED MOTOR,
ELECTRICAL EQUIPMENT,
OVERHEAD TROLLEY,
AND CHASSIS
ARE ALL
CONSTRUCTED AT OUR
LONDON WORKS.

OVER
1,200,000
CAR MILES RUN;
THE AVERAGE COST
OF RUNNING HAS BEEN
UNDER 5d.
PER CAR MILE.

'Cedes' System in London.

Full Particulars from
Chief Office: 112, GT. PORTLAND STREET, LONDON, W.

KEIGHLEY TRANSPOR
1921

A - DEPÔT (WEST OF ROAD)
B - MALSIS RD.
C - PARK AVENUE
D - GOULBOURNE ST.
E - VICTORIA RD.
F - INSTITUTE
G - CAVENDISH ST.
H - THE CROSS
I - ST. JOHN'S RD.

INSET 1
OVERHEAD LINE
DETAILS
TRAMCAR
TRACKLESS

INSET 2

EXPERIMENTAL 'BUS ROUTES IN THE
HIGHFIELD AREA 1910-11
(SEE TEXT)

TRAMWAYS   TRACKLESS ROU
FORMERLY MOTOR-BUS (EXCEPT "E" AND THE LEES TO OXENHOPE SECTION
FORMER MOTOR-BUS ROUTES, NEVER TRACKLESS
RAILWAYS   BOUNDARIES

JSK 8/64

INGROW TERMINUS

52.   Cedes-Stoll railless vehicles serviced three outlying routes from 1913, the first of which was Ingrow to Cross Roads, later extended to Oxenhope. Here the experimental Austrian built No. 0 is seen on trial, just leaving Ingrow terminus. Note the balcony tram at the terminus, and an open topped motorbus on the right, with St John's Church on the eminence behind. The vehicle reputedly bore a red and blue livery.

CROSS ROADS

53.   A frontal view of the Cedes single deck, front entrance, 24-seater, taken looking east along Haworth Road, Lees, with Lees Primary School visible on the far left. The neat looking wall on the right is still in existence.

54.   The Cedes car is here seen at the 1913 Cross Roads terminus at the junction of Lees
Lane and Hebden Road, with Leaf Street behind the car. The shot shows clearly the 25lb/11.3kg
four-wheel trolley running along the overhead wires. The metal pendulum adjusted the tension of
the trolley on the wiring, whilst the flexible cable was wound onto a drum under the bonnet. The
disadvantages of the system are clearly apparent. The trolleys were sometimes wont to fall off the
wires, and occasionally broke free of their cables, racing away along the overhead and leaving the
cars stranded!

OAKWORTH

55.   The Oakworth service was the second to commence operations in late 1914, but photographic coverage of the route is sparse. This post World War I view shows renumbered Cedes Car 58 ascending Lidget Hill, Oakworth on its return to Keighley on a 16th August 1921 trial after the trackless had been fitted with a front wheel drive. Note the lightweight Cedes pole on the left, and the good view of the over-running trolley and pendulum.

UTLEY TERMINUS

56.   The last Cedes line was to Sutton-in-Craven and opened in early 1915. A corrugated iron shed was built on St John's Road, Utley to house the cars servicing this route. It was erected at a cost of £500, plus £372 for the necessary land.

57.   Cedes Car 4, one of the 9 Dodson bodied 29-seater tracklesses, is here pictured at Utley in 1919 in front of a balcony tram at the terminus, and just about to set out for Sutton.

58.   The same trolleybus is pictured a little further along Skipton Road, obviously on the same wet day, with St John's Road on the left. Behind the car, note the Cedes heavy lattice pole, which marks the start of the Sutton wiring.

59.   Further towards Keighley, at the very end of the tramline, an unidentified Cedes trolleybus prepares to execute a U-turn using the width of Ferncliffe Drive on the left to assist with the revolution. The two initial Cedes traction poles can be seen in the distance, together with the depot wiring, the only overhead junction on the whole Cedes system.

60.   An interesting shot of the turning car whose rear platform step is practically scraping the
road surface, as the conductress on the rear platform warily watches the photographer. The extreme
length of the flexible cable enabled these vehicles to execute some surprising manoeuvres. Note
that the tram-trolleybus wiring was connected end on, and the hangar-like fitting on the overhead
allowed the trolley to run through the junction. By contrast with the trams, the Corporation logo
was painted on the waist panel of the trolleybuses.

61.   Cedes Tracklesses 4 and 6 meet at Hawkcliffe, just east of Steeton in this 1915 image. The contractors had only strung one pair of running wires along the route, so the vehicles had to exchange trolleys when they met. The conductor waves a red flag to warn approaching traffic, whilst the drivers swap cables. Note the line of light traction poles carrying the overhead on the right.

SUTTON-IN-CRAVEN

62.   In 1916 Keighley purchased the first ever double deck trolleybus, a 33-seater built by Cedes and used in trials at Hove. They ran it initially in blue and white colours, and clumsily painted out the Hove logo and coat-of-arms. This singular vehicle is seen in service at the Sutton terminus in 1919. Top deck passengers were reportedly terrified when the trolley passed overhead, fearful of being clouted by the pendulum. Whilst on the level and up inclines, the trolley was towed behind the bus, but whilst descending hills it shot disconcertingly forward ahead of the car!

THE KEIGHLEY TROLLEYBUSES

FLEET VEHICLES

63.   The first four trolleybuses were single deck front entrance Strakers with Dodson bodies like No.3, rescued from the ex-Cedes buses. They were delivered in early September and Straker 3 is pictured here at Utley Chapel. Note the Estler trolleybases, and the shelter on the right, erected at the terminus in 1918.

64.   The first four single deckers were followed by six Brush bodied double deck Strakers like No.5, here seen at the Brush works, and delivered in mid-November. The solid tyred 9 ton vehicles seated 50 riders, and though state-of-the-art when new, they were soon dated by the continuous development in trolleybus design. Note the destination, CROSS ROADS, to which the vehicles never went.

65.　　　Photographs were taken of several of the interiors of the double deckers. Here the lower saloon of Straker 12, looking forward, can be appreciated, with its 24-seat capacity and plywood seats. Both decks had ample headroom, suiting the taller passengers.

66.　　　The insides of Straker 10 were pictured at Ingrow in late 1924. This view shows the lower deck looking to the rear. Riders sitting here enjoyed the privilege of padded cushions and seat backs. The window bills advertise a whist drive and dance at the Baths Hall on 16th December, and Christmas holiday traffic schedules.

67.   We observe the top deck of the same car, again looking to the rear. The 26 passengers here endured more Spartan riding, with slatted seats embodying hard plywood backs.

68.   An excellent side view depicts Straker 13 at the Brush works. This 32-seat trolleybus entered service in December 1924. Note the front entrance with its folding door, and the revised paint scheme applied to all these vehicles.

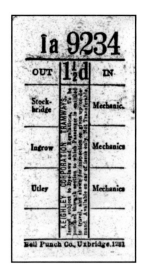

(G.Croughton coll.)

These four tickets were rescued from Straker 5 during its restoration.

½d (pink)   1½d (yellow)

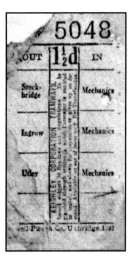

1d (buff)   1d (buff)

69.　　　Straker 5 took part in an early test run. Councillors and officials are here seen mounting the vehicle at the South Street depot. The steep staircases were likened to the biblical Jacob's Ladder, whilst the open backs of the cars led them to be christened 'the Iceboxes.'

UTLEY TERMINUS

70.   'Oh what a tangled web…' The overhead was revamped at the Utley depot in 1924 to allow for twin sets of wires, and this vista shows one of the single deckers on the junction leading into the enlarged St John's Road car shed. In the near distance a double decker heads for town.

71.   In much the same place, Straker 3 noses out into Skipton Road using the 360 degree traverse allowed by the Estler trolleybases. Note the twin Cedes traction poles in the foreground, and the abandoned wiring of the Sutton Cedes system heading away into the distance.

72.   The tall, boxy lines of Straker 5 show up well in this view as the trackless poses at the entrance to Utley Depot. Note the piano-like streamlining below the top saloon windows, and the advertisements now being applied to the upper surfaces of the car.

73.   Straker 2 picks up traffic at the Utley bus shelter, opposite the Ferncliffe Road rise on a damp and wet day, whilst driver and conductor take the last chance for a casual chat.

74.   This is a good view of Straker 8, on the Stockbridge run, taken at the same venue, but from the opposite direction. The 15ft 7in/4.7 metres height of these vehicles (to the trolleybases) is immediately apparent. The driver is in uniform, though the conductor, perhaps a trainee, remains in civvies.

75.   Straker 9 is observed at the same spot, and again Stockbridge bound, with driver, conductor and inspector all posing for their photograph. Ferncliffe Road climbs away to the left, and the stop sign shows up well by the shelter to the right.

SKIPTON ROAD

76.   Straker 9 again, halts opposite the Roebuck Inn, whilst a 'pirate' single deck motor bus runs by. Note the Shell petrol advert by the public house – 'for the utmost horse power.' A scrap merchant pulls his laden cart towards town, whilst the character sitting below the advertising board is presumably waiting for the hostelry to open!

77.   Single-deck Strakers 13 and 12 stop by Cliffe Castle gates in this 1924 winter scene to have their picture taken. No. 12 is bound for Stockbridge, and the image reveals good detail of the running wire at this point. Note the feeder cable boosting power to the positive wires from the right.

NORTH STREET

→

79.　　Strakers 8 and 7 await trade on opposite sides of a thinly populated North Street in December 1924. Note the Regent Picture House on the left, whose premises are now occupied by the more prosaically named Vanilla Bar. Unfortunately the cinema's offering that week is not clear enough to read!

78.　　One of the double deckers is shown on the corner of North and Cavendish Streets, with the Institute looming in the background. The pristine state of the bus suggests the image was taken early in the trackless era.

→

80.　　Between 4th and 11th July 1925 a prototype Garrett 37-seat, single deck, centre entrance railless was demonstrated at Keighley. The big, squared off vehicle with a red and white Roe body and mounted on pneumatic tyres, is here seen opposite the Institute. It was the first trolleybus ever built by the firm, and its more advanced lines show how quickly new trackless designs were appearing.

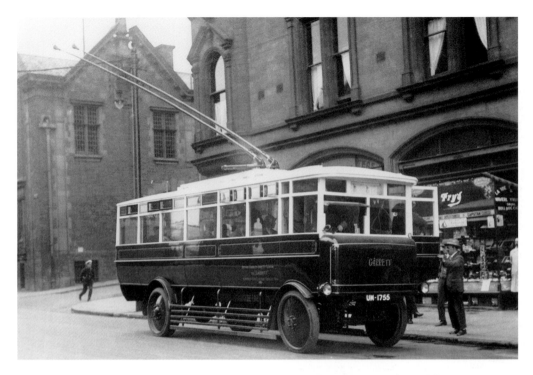

81.　　The big Garrett is here shown from the opposite direction, with the public library on the left and Albert Street behind the rear of the car. The building behind the trackless is now a branch of Wetherspoons. Note the abreast pairing of the trolleybooms in contrast with the Estlers which were mounted one above the other on a central spindle.

82.　　Straker 5 heads for the South Street depot along the southern part of North Street, with Spencer Street just to the right of the vehicle. Note that at least one set of tram tracks was still in situ when this view was taken.

CHURCH STREET

83.	Cedes Car 58 (re-numbered from 8 in 1920), waits outside the Devonshire Arms (now the Korner Bar) on 16th August 1921, whilst on a trial to Oakworth.

84.   Straker 18, the last of the batch of Brush trolleybuses, heads along the outward route to Ingrow on 25th June 1931. It is hotly pursued by a Corporation Leyland Titan bound for Haworth.

HIGH STREET

85.   On the same day as the last illustration, Straker 8 moves east down High Street, and is just about to turn left into North Street on the way to Utley. Church Street is on the right, and Uncle Chadwick's shop – 'the peoples' outfitter and clothier' - on the left featured in advertisements on the trackless.

86.   Looking in the opposite direction, Cedes Car 7 awaits passengers at the terminus for Oakworth. No.7 was one of the last of the Cedes batch, and had a more powerful motor to cope with the hillier routes. The building above the trolleybus, with its ornate Egyptian style frontage, survives as Jean Junction, though the buildings in the distance have all been swept away for the roundabout which now occupies the site.

87.   Cedes Car 58 again, turning into High Street from North Street on its way to Oakworth on 16th August 1921. The vehicle had been adapted for front wheel drive, but it was not a success. Its steering was very heavy, and it reputedly needed 36 revolutions of the steering wheel to turn the car at the termini!

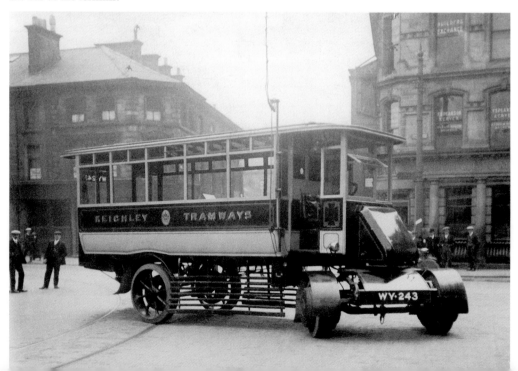

INGROW TERMINUS

88.   A rear view of Straker 10 at Ingrow, was probably taken on the occasion when the interiors were photographed in December 1924. The indicator box reads SPECIAL CAR. Note the securing hooks for holding the lowered booms, visible above the rear window of the trackless.

89.   This publicity shot of the same car was taken at the same time as the last. An admiring audience can be seen on the left, and the tower of St John's can just be seen above the trolleybooms. The window bill advertises the whist drive and dance seen in picture 66.

90.   Special Car 12, again pictured at Ingrow, shows the closed hinged frontal door common to the batch. Though the double deckers were known as the 'Iceboxes' the single deckers by comparison were said, in warm weather, to have 'all the advantages of a Turkish bath without the accompanying rub-down.'

91.　　　Straker 10 cosies up to Leyland Titan TD1 (No.53) at Ingrow. The latter, new in August 1928, was on its way to Fell Lane. The height differences between the two vehicles can be well appreciated in this view. With a height of only 13ft/3.9 metres the upper-deck headroom on the Leylands was very cramped in comparison with the trolleybuses, which already look very dated.

92.   One of the Cedes tracklesses heads out from the Ingrow depot onto the end of Halifax Road, presumably on its way to Cross Roads. Again, we get a good view of the trolley, cable and pendulum weight. On the right passengers have eschewed the shelter to await the tram to town. The glazed structure behind the car can still be seen.

93.   The 1925 Garrett prototype is here seen at the Ingrow turning loop. Running off to the right is the overhead for the Cedes-Stoll system for the Cross Roads route, which remained in use until 3rd May 1926.

CAVENDISH STREET

94.	Looking west at the top of the street facing the public library, the details of the running wire at this point are well picked up against the skyline. Both sets of lines allowed trolley vehicles either to turn left for Ingrow, or right for Utley.

95.   Straker 6 waits at the Stockbridge barrier at the top of the street, alongside the Institute. The façade of the United Methodist Free Church rises above Guy motorbuses 37 and 42, which are en route for Bingley.

96.   Straker 15 waits at the same barrier. No.15 was the first of the final batch of three, which arrived in August 1925. This allowed most of the 1-4 series trolleybuses to be withdrawn. Initially the fleet numbers were only carried on the front dash panel, but they gradually appeared on the cab sides, as seen here. Manager, Clement Jackson, had resigned in July, and these vehicles duly bore the name of his successor, Ronald Fearnley.

97.   A picturesque view of a leafy Town Hall Square, taken from a Town Hall window, shows the fine and elegant War Memorial together with two single deck Tilling-Stevens motorbuses, and, on the right, a Leyland Titan, all in the service of West Yorkshire. In the near distance a double deck Straker heads off for Stockbridge. The photograph depicts the well proportioned United Methodist Church, pulled down in the 1960s for a featureless replacement, part of Keighley Technical College.

98.   Straker 6 ascends the gentle incline west up Cavendish Street in this late 1920s scene. On the left are the well known series of glass verandas shading the north side of the thoroughfare.

BRADFORD ROAD

99.   Straker 17, followed by another unidentified double decker, passes Corporation motorbuses Guy 42 and Leyland 21 outside the Queen's Hotel (now Richard Craven Electricals) and situated on the corner of Dalton Lane. The parked vehicles are awaiting workmen from Prince, Smith and Son's manufacturers lower down the road.

100.   Further down Bradford Road and outside Prince, Smith's works, Corporation trolleybuses await the factory workforce. The double decker on the left is on its way to Stockbridge whilst single deck Straker 14 is Utley bound. Straker 5 is on the Ingrow run. A West Yorkshire Leyland Lion heads past the waiting electric vehicles.

101.   Outside Prince, Smith's works on 4th July 1925, Tramway Committee members and other officials pose in front of the Garrett demonstrator at the start of its Keighley sojourn. The short, bowler-hatted figure at the centre of the group is manager Clement Jackson, who was very shortly to depart to a post in South Africa.

102.   Along a cobbled Bradford Road, Straker 18, on its way to Ingrow, edges past a fallen tree opposite Victoria Park. Judging from the illustration, a considerable backup of cars and buses are following the trackless.

STOCKBRIDGE TERMINUS

103.   Straker 16 halts near the junction with Cornwall Road after the abandonment of the turning circle during the rebuilding of the Stock Bridge in 1929. The loop was replaced by a reverser located some 88 yards/80.4 metres nearer to Keighley.

104.   Further back towards the bridge Straker 7 and two single deckers (count the trolleybooms), await trade for Utley and Stockbridge. At the top left can be seen the reverser situated at the end of Cornwall Road.

105.   Taken from the opposite direction, Straker 16, together with crew and a few riders, pose in front of the Ingrow bound vehicle. The wiring for Cornwall Road reverser can be seen above and to the left of the bus. The site of the original turning loop was at Ferrand's Garage, visible on the left of the picture, just in front of the distant bridge.

106.   A good shot of Straker 6 at the original
terminus at the start of the trackless service,
shows the open nature of the area in 1924. The
forecourt of Ferrand's Garage, which formed
part of the turning circle, can be seen on the left.
The uncompromisingly boxy lines of the buses
can be well appreciated in this photograph.

107.   This image of Straker 6, at the
windswept terminus with the bridge behind,
also contains an excellent view of the wiring
of the turning circle above the bus. The garage
forecourt, a necessary part of the U-turn, can be
seen to the left.

108.   Straker 18 is here seen manoeuvring round the loop, an operation often referred to
as 'the long heave-ho' or 'swing-around' and likened by some drivers with the docking of an
Atlantic liner! Cranes and other paraphernalia on the left show that rebuilding of the bridge has
just commenced.

LAST DAY OF THE TRACKLESS

109.   A large crowd congregates at the Institute at 11pm on the evening of 31st August 1932
for the last official trolleybus journey, using Straker 17. The Mayor, Alderman M.P.Cryer (in
peaked cap), acted as driver. Alderman Albert Smith (Chairman of the Tramways Committee) on
his left undertook the conducting duties. The manager, Herbert Binns, can be seen under the UT
of UTLEY on the Titan TD2 motorbus (No.58) on the left.

110.   One of the last of the Utley service trolleybuses (15 or 17) lines up with Titan 58 in front of a diverse throng, which includes a police constable, complete with bullseye lamp, on the left. The bespectacled figure of Herbert Binns stands to the right of the Leyland badge on the radiator of the motorbus.

111.   The Last Hurrah took place at the Roebuck Inn, Utley, when the final official bus reached the terminus. The trolleybus was packed with passengers hanging on to any part of the vehicle within their grasp. Various car crews complete the ensemble, as they pose for the cameraman in one of the very last shots taken of a memorable night.

112.   Almost certainly the last trolleybus to enter the Utley depot was Straker 15, seen here with crews, officials and riders. The vehicle was photographed by St John's Road on the right, marked by the Cedes lattice pole visible in the background.

113.   Car crews and Utley Depot staff line up in front of the last two electric service vehicles to enter the car shed, on the night of 31st August. Straker 16 is on the left and 15 on the right.

SURVIVORS

114.　　　Single deck Straker 12 was one of the two tracklesses to avoid dismantling or scrapping. It is here pictured on a site off Aireworth Road in the mid-1950s. In 1988 it was removed to the Beamish Open Air Museum for preservation.

115.   Straker 5 was taken to Skirethorns near Grassington and served as a holiday home for many years. It was rescued in 1969 and spent some years in Peter Black's Museum in Keighley, before its relocation to the Keighley Bus Museum in 2000. This view was taken in February 1967.

116.   Straker 12 is seen here at Beamish Open Air Museum in May 1989, after its removal from Grassington. The rear axle can be seen alongside the body of the trolleybus.

117.   Straker 5 is pictured in the yard of Richard Craven's premises on Dalton Lane during its removal to the Keighley Bus Museum.

118.   The venerable trolleybus is here shown being towed into the Museum premises in February 2000.

119.   The trackless enters its new home in its restored livery, though lacking its original trolleybooms.

120.   The Straker-Clough nameplate is still visible at the base of the dash panel of the preserved vehicle.

MP Middleton Press

EVOLVING THE ULTIMATE RAIL ENCYCLOPEDIA

Easebourne Lane, Midhurst, West Sussex.
GU29 9AZ   Tel:01730 813169

www.middletonpress.co.uk   email:info@middletonpress.co.uk

A-0 906520   B-1 873793   C-1 901706   D-1 904474

OOP Out of Print at time of printing - Please check current availability   **BROCHURE AVAILABLE SHOWING NEW TITLES**

A
Abergavenny to Merthyr C 91 5
Aldgate & Stepney Tramways B 70 7
Allhallows - Branch Line to A 62 2
Alton - Branch Lines to A 11 8
Andover to Southampton A 82 7
Ascot - Branch Lines around A 64 9
Ashburton - Branch Line to B 95 2
Ashford - Steam to Eurostar B 67 7
Ashford to Dover A 48 7
Austrian Narrow Gauge D 04 7
Avonmouth - BL around D 42 X
B
Banbury to Birmingham D 27 6
Barking to Southend C 80 X
Barnet & Finchley Tramways B 93 6
Barry - Branch Lines around D 50 0
Basingstoke to Salisbury A 89 4
Bath Green Park to Bristol C 36 2
Bath to Evercreech Junction A 60 6
Bath Tramways B 86 3
Battle over Portsmouth 1940 A 29 0
Battle over Sussex 1940 A 79 7
Bedford to Wellingborough D 31 4
Betwixt Petersfield & Midhurst A 94 0
Blitz over Sussex 1941-42 B 35 9
Bodmin - Branch Lines around B 83 9
Bognor at War 1939-45 B 59 6
Bombers over Sussex 1943-45 B 51 0
Bournemouth & Poole Trys B 47 2
Bournemouth to Evercreech Jn A 46 0
Bournemouth to Weymouth A 57 2
Bournemouth Trolleybuses C 10 9
Bradford Trolleybuses D 19 5
Brecon to Neath D 43 8
Brecon to Newport D 16 0
Brickmaking in Sussex B 19 7
Brightons Tramways B 02 2 OOP
Brighton to Eastbourne A 16 9
Brighton to Worthing A 03 7
Brighton Trolleybuses D 34 9
Bristols Tramways B 57 X
Bristol to Taunton D 03 9
Bromley South to Rochester B 23 5
Bromsgrove to Gloucester D 73 X
Brunel - A railtour of his achievements D 74 8
Bude - Branch Line to B 29 4
Burnham to Evercreech Jn A 68 1
Burton & Ashby Tramways C 51 6
C
Camberwell & West Norwood Tys B 22 7
Cambridge to Ely D 55 1
Canterbury - Branch Lines around B 58 8
Cardiff Trolleybuses D 64 0
Caterham & Tattenham Corner B 25 1
Changing Midhurst C 15 X
Chard and Yeovil - BLs around C 30 3
Charing Cross to Dartford A 75 4
Charing Cross to Orpington A 96 7
Cheddar - Branch Line to B 90 1
Cheltenham to Andover C 43 5
Cheltenham to Redditch D 81 0
Chesterfield Tramways D 37 3
Chesterfield Trolleybuses D 51 9
Chichester to Portsmouth A 14 2
Clapham & Streatham Trys B 97 9 OOP
Clapham Junction - 50 yrs C 06 0 OOP
Clapham Junction to Beckenham Jn B 36 7
Clevedon & Portishead - BLs to D 18 7
Collectors Trains, Trolleys & Trams D 29 2
Colonel Stephens D62 4
Cornwall Narrow Gauge D 56 X
Crawley to Littlehampton A 34 7
Cromer - Branch Lines around C 26 5
Croydons Tramways B 42 1
Croydons Trolleybuses B 73 1 OOP
Croydon to East Grinstead B 48 0
Crystal Palace (HL) & Catford Loop A 87 8
D
Darlington Trolleybuses D 33 0
Dartford to Sittingbourne B 34 0
Derby Tramways D 17 9
Derby Trolleybuses C 72 9
Derwent Valley - Branch Line to the D 06 3
Didcot to Banbury D 02 0
Didcot to Swindon C 84 2
Didcot to Winchester C 13 3
Dorset & Somerset Narrow Gauge D 76 4
Douglas to Peel C 88 5
Douglas to Port Erin C 55 9
Douglas to Ramsey D 39 X
Dovers Tramways B 24 3
Dover to Ramsgate A 78 9

E
Ealing to Slough C 42 7
Eastbourne to Hastings A 27 4
East Cornwall Mineral Railways D 22 5
East Croydon to Three Bridges A 53 3
East Grinstead - Branch Lines to A 07 X
East Ham & West Ham Tramways B 52 9
East Kent Light Railway A 61 4 OOP
East London - Branch Lines of C 44 3
East London Line B 80 4
East Ridings Secret Resistance D 21 7
Edgware & Willesden Tramways C 18 4
Effingham Junction - BLs around A 74 6
Eltham & Woolwich Tramways B 74 X OOP
Ely to Kings Lynn C 53 2
Ely to Norwich C 90 7
Embankment & Waterloo Tramways B 41 3
Enfield & Wood Green Trys C 03 6 OOP
Enfield Town & Palace Gates - BL to D 32 2
Epsom to Horsham A 30 4
Euston to Harrow & Wealdstone C 89 3
Exeter & Taunton Tramways B 32 4
Exeter to Barnstaple B 15 4
Exeter to Newton Abbot C 49 4
Exeter to Tavistock B 69 3
Exmouth - Branch Lines to B 00 6
F
Fairford - Branch Line to A 52 5
Falmouth, Helston & St. Ives - BL to C 74 5
Fareham to Salisbury A 67 3
Faversham to Dover B 05 7
Felixstowe & Aldeburgh - BL to D 20 9
Fenchurch Street to Barking C 20 6
Festiniog - 50 yrs of enterprise C 83 4
Festiniog in the Fifties B 68 5
Festiniog in the Sixties B 91 X
Finsbury Park to Alexandra Palace C 02 8
Frome to Bristol B 77 4
Fulwell - Trams, Trolleys & Buses B 11 X
G
Gloucester to Bristol D 35 7
Gloucester to Cardiff D 66 7
Gosport & Horndean Trys B 92 8
Gosport - Branch Lines around A 36 3
Great Yarmouth Tramways D 13 6
Greece Narrow Gauge D 72 1
Greenwich & Dartford Tramways B 14 6 OOP
Guildford to Redhill A 63 0
H
Hammersmith & Hounslow Trys C 33 8
Hampshire Narrow Gauge D 36 5
Hampshire Waterways A 84 3 OOP
Hampstead & Highgate Tramways B 53 7
Harrow to Watford D 14 4
Hastings to Ashford A 37 1 OOP
Hastings Tramways B 18 9
Hastings Trolleybuses B 81 2 OOP
Hawkhurst - Branch Line to A 66 5
Hayling - Branch Line to A 12 6
Haywards Heath to Seaford A 28 2
Henley, Windsor & Marlow - BL to C77 X
Hereford to Newport D 54 3
Hexham to Carlisle D 75 6
Hitchin to Peterborough D 07 1
Holborn & Finsbury Tramways B 79 0
Holborn Viaduct to Lewisham A 81 9
Horsham - Branch Lines to A 02 9
Huddersfield Trolleybuses C 92 3
Hull Tramways D60 8
Hull Trolleybuses D 24 1
Huntingdon - Branch Lines around A 93 2
I
Ilford & Barking Tramways B 61 8
Ilford to Shenfield C 97 4
Ilfracombe - Branch Line to B 21 9
Ilkeston & Glossop Tramways D 40 3
Industrial Rlys of the South East A 09 6
Ipswich to Saxmundham C 41 9
Ipswich Trolleybuses D 59 4
Isle of Wight Lines - 50 yrs C 12 5
K
Kent & East Sussex Waterways A 72 X
Kent Narrow Gauge C 45 1
Kent Seaways - Hoys to Hovercraft D 79 9
Kingsbridge - Branch Line to C 98 2
Kingston & Hounslow Loops A 83 5 OOP
Kingston & Wimbledon Tramways B 56 1
Kingswear - Branch Line to C 17 6
L
Lambourn - Branch Line to C 70 2
Launceston & Princetown - BL to C 19 2
Lewisham & Catford Tramways B 26 X OOP
Lewisham to Dartford A 92 4

Lines around Wimbledon B 75 8
Liverpool Street to Chingford D 01 2
Liverpool Street to Ilford C 34 6
Liverpool Tramways - Eastern C 04 4
Liverpool Tramways - Northern C 46 X
Liverpool Tramways - Southern C 23 0
London Bridge to Addiscombe B 20 0
London Bridge to East Croydon A 58 4
London Chatham & Dover Railway A 88 6
London Termini - Past and Proposed D 00 4
London to Portsmouth Waterways B 43 X
Longmoor - Branch Lines to A 41 X
Looe - Branch Line to C 22 2
Lyme Regis - Branch Line to A 45 2
Lynton - Branch Line to B 04 9
M
Maidstone & Chatham Tramways B 40 5
Maidstone Trolleybuses C 00 1 OOP
March - Branch Lines around B 09 X
Margate & Ramsgate Tramways C 52 4
Marylebone to Rickmansworth D49 7
Midhurst - Branch Lines around A 49 5
Midhurst - Branch Lines to A 01 0 OOP
Military Defence of West Sussex A 23 1
Military Signals, South Coast C 54 0
Minehead - Branch Line to A 80 2
Mitcham Junction Lines B 01 4
Mitchell & company C 59 1
Monmouthshire Eastern Valleys D 71 3
Moreton-in-Marsh to Worcester D 26 8
Moretonhampstead - BL to C 27 3
Mountain Ash to Neath D 80 2
N
Newbury to Westbury C 66 4
Newcastle to Hexham D 69 1
Newcastle Trolleybuses D 78 0
Newport (IOW) - Branch Lines to A 26 6
Newquay - Branch Lines to C 71 0
Newton Abbot to Plymouth C 60 5
Northern France Narrow Gauge C 75 3
North East German Narrow Gauge D 44 6
North Kent Tramways B 44 8
North London Line B 94 4
North Woolwich - BLs around C 65 6
Norwich Tramways C 40 0
Nottinghamshire & Derbyshire T/B D 63 2
Nottinghamshire & Derbyshire T/W D 53 5
O
Orpington to Tonbridge B 03 0 OOP
Oxford to Bletchley D57 8
Oxford to Moreton-in-Marsh D 15 2
P
Paddington to Ealing C 37 0
Paddington to Princes Risborough C 81 8
Padstow - Branch Line to B 54 5
Plymouth - BLs around B 98 7
Plymouth to St. Austell C 63 X
Pontypool to Mountain Ash D 65 9
Porthmadog 1954-94 - BL around B 31 6
Porthmadog to Blaenau B 50 2 OOP
Portmadoc 1923-46 - BL around B 13 8
Portsmouths Tramways B 72 3
Portsmouth to Southampton A 31 2
Portsmouth Trolleybuses C 73 7
Potters Bar to Cambridge D 70 5
Princes Risborough - Branch Lines to D 05 5
Princes Risborough to Banbury C 85 0
R
Railways to Victory C 16 8/7 OOP
Reading to Basingstoke B 27 8
Reading to Didcot C 79 6
Reading to Guildford A 47 9 OOP
Reading Tramways B 87 1
Reading Trolleybuses C 05 2
Redhill to Ashford A 73 8
Return to Blaenau 1970-82 C 64 8
Rickmansworth to Aylesbury D 61 6
Roman Roads of Hampshire D 67 5
Roman Roads of Surrey C 61 3
Roman Roads of Sussex C 48 6
Romneyrail C 32 X
Ryde to Ventnor A 19 3
S
Salisbury to Westbury B 39 1
Salisbury to Yeovil B 06 5 OOP
Saxmundham to Yarmouth C 69 9
Saxony Narrow Gauge D 47 0
Seaton & Eastbourne Tramways B 76 6 OOP
Seaton & Sidmouth - Branch Lines to A 95 9
Secret Sussex Resistance B 82 0
SECR Centenary album C 11 7
Selsey - Branch Line to A 04 5
Sheerness - Branch Lines around B 16 2

Shepherds Bush to Uxbridge T/Ws C 28 1
Shrewsbury - Branch Line to A 86 X
Sierra Leone Narrow Gauge D 28 4
Sittingbourne to Ramsgate A 90 8
Slough to Newbury C 56 7
Solent - Creeks, Crafts & Cargoes D 52 7
Southamptons Tramways B 33 2
Southampton to Bournemouth A 42 8
Southend-on-Sea Tramways A 88 8
Southern France Narrow Gauge C 47 8
Southwark & Deptford Tramways B 38 3
Southwold - Branch Line to A 15 0
South Eastern & Chatham Railways C 08\
South London Line B 46 4
South London Tramways 1903-33 D 10 1
St. Albans to Bedford D 08 X
St. Austell to Penzance C 67 2
St. Pancras to Barking D 68 3
St. Pancras to St. Albans C 78 8
Stamford Hill Tramways B 85 5
Steaming through Cornwall B 30 8 OOP
Steaming through Kent A 13 4 OOP
Steaming through the Isle of Wight A 56 8\
Steaming through West Hants A 69 X
Stratford upon avon to Birmingham D 77\
Stratford upon Avon to Cheltenham C 25\
Strood to Paddock Wood B 12 X
Surrey Home Guard C 57 5
Surrey Narrow Gauge C 87 7
Surrey Waterways A 51 7 OOP
Sussex Home Guard C 24 9
Sussex Narrow Gauge C 68 0
Sussex Shipping Sail, Steam & Motor D 2\
Swanley to Ashford B 45 6
Swindon to Bristol C 96 6
Swindon to Gloucester D36 2
Swindon to Newport D 30 6
Swiss Narrow Gauge C 94 X
T
Talyllyn - 50 years C 39 7
Taunton to Barnstaple B 60 X
Taunton to Exeter C 82 6
Tavistock to Plymouth B 88 X
Tees-side Trolleybuses D 58 6
Tenterden - Branch Line to A 21 5
Thanet's Tramways B 11 1 OOP
Three Bridges to Brighton A 35 5
Tilbury Loop C 86 9
Tiverton - Branch Lines around C 62 1
Tivetshall to Beccles D 41 1
Tonbridge to Hastings A 44 4
Torrington - Branch Lines to B 37 5
Tunbridge Wells - Branch Lines to A 32 0
Twickenham & Kingston Trys C 35 4
Two-Foot Gauge Survivors C 21 4 OOP
U
Upwell - Branch Line to B 64 2
V
Victoria & Lambeth Tramways B 49 9
Victoria to Bromley South A 98 3
Victoria to East Croydon A 40 1 OOP
Vivarais C 31 1
W
Walthamstow & Leyton Tramways B 65 \
Waltham Cross & Edmonton Trys C 07 9\
Wandsworth & Battersea Tramways B 63\
Wantage - Branch Line to D 25 X
Wareham to Swanage - 50 yrs D 09 8
War on the Line A 10 X
Waterloo to Windsor A 54 1
Waterloo to Woking A 38 X
Watford to Leighton Buzzard D 45 4
Wenford Bridge to Fowey C 09 5
Westbury to Bath B 55 3
Westbury to Taunton C 76 3
West Cornwall Mineral Railways D 48 9
West Croydon to Epsom B 08 1
West London - Branch Lines of C 50 8
West London Line B 84 7
West Sussex Waterways A 24 X OOP
West Wiltshire - Branch Lines of D 12 8
Weymouth - Branch Lines around A 65 7
Willesden Junction to Richmond B 71 5
Wimbledon to Beckenham C 58 3
Wimbledon to Epsom B 62 6
Wimborne - Branch Lines around A 97 5
Wisbech - Branch Lines around C 01 X
Wisbech 1800-1901 C 93 1
Woking to Altor. A 59 2
Woking to Portsmouth A 25 8
Woking to Southampton A 55 X
Woolwich & Dartford Trolleys B 66 9 OO\
Worcester to Hereford D 38 1
Worthing to Chichester A 06 1
Y
Yeovil - 50 yrs change C 38 9
Yeovil to Dorchester A 76 2 OOP
Yeovil to Exeter A 91 6
York Tramways & Trolleybuses D 82 9